Creature Features

Creature Noses

nicola
whittaker

First published in 2001 by
Franklin Watts
96 Leonard Street
London
WC2A 4XD

Franklin Watts Australia
56 O'Riordan Street
Alexandria
NSW 2015

Editor: Samantha Armstrong
Designer: Jason Anscomb
Science consultant: Dr Jim Flegg

ISBN: 0 7496 4028 6
Dewey Decimal Number: 591.1
A CIP number for this book is available from the British Library

Picture credits:
NHPA: 4 Martin Harvey; 5 E.A. Janes; 6-7 Pavel German;
8-9 Martin Harvey; 10-11 and cover Gerard Lacz;
12-13 Jany Sauvanet; 15 Gerard Lacz; 16 A.N.T.;
17 Joe Blossom; 18/19 Daniel Heuclin; 18-19 and cover Martin
Harvey; 20 E.A. Janes; 21 and cover Jean-Louis Le Moigne.
Oxford Scientific Films: 14 Zig Leszczynski.
Planet Earth Pictures: 24-25 Ken Lucas.
Still Pictures: 22-23 Fritz Polking.
Franklin Watts Photo Library: 26-27.
Printed in Hong Kong/China

Creature Features

Creature Noses

nicola whittaker

W
FRANKLIN WATTS
LONDON·SYDNEY

Different creatures

have different noses.

Some are small,

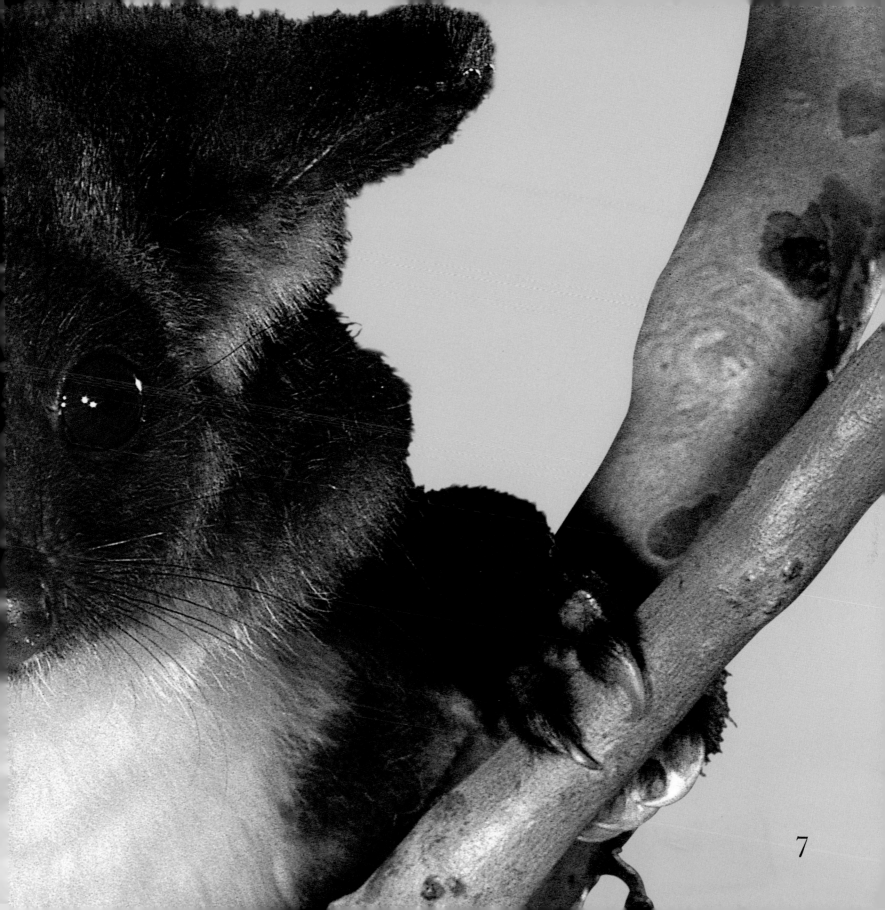

some
are
strong.

Some are

bold,

11

this one hides a tongue!

Some noses feel,

some follow Scent.

15

Some noses are

pointed,

others are bent!

Some noses

18

hunt...

this nose

can close

tight.

This nose

has a

ring,

this one is bright.

Some
noses

hide?

some noses stick Out!

24

But I think my nose is the

best nose about!

27

Glossary

Galapagos Giant Tortoise
(Geochelone elephantopus)
Reptile (tortoise family)
Lives: Galapagos Islands in
the Pacific Ocean
Eats: Plants
Can grow up to 1 metre long.

Pig
(Sus scrofa)
Mammal (pig family)
Lives: Worldwide
Eats: Anything
Farm animals, domesticated
from wild ancestors.

Greater Honeyglider
(Petauroides volans)
Marsupial (pouched mammal)
Lives: Australia
Eats: Nectar
Skin flaps under its arms and
legs let it glide between trees.

African Elephant
(Loxodonta africana)
Mammal (elephant family)
Lives: Africa
Eats: Plants
Uses its muscular trunk to
pick up bundles of plants.

Mandrill
(Mandrillus sphinx)
Mammal (monkey family)
Lives: West African forests
Eats: Almost anything
The male's bright nose
scares away other males.

Giant Anteater
(Myrmecophaga tridactyla)
Mammal (sloth and anteater family)
Lives: South America
Eats: Ants and termites
Its long nose has a tiny
mouth at the end.

Star-Nosed Mole
(Condylura cristata)
Mammal (mole family)
Lives: North America
Eats: Worms and insects
The feelers on its nose help it
find its way underground.

Bloodhound
(Canis familiaris)
Mammal (dog family)
Lives: Most countries
Eats: Most things
Specially bred to have a
wonderful sense of smell.

Features

29

Glossary

Elephant Shark
(Callorhynchus milii)
Fish (marine shark family)
Lives: Oceans near Australia
Eats: Fish
Uses its sensitive nose to find prey, even hidden in the sand.

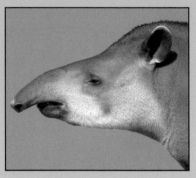

Tapir
(Tapir terrestris)
Mammal (horse family)
Lives: South American and Malayan forests
Eats: Leaves
Uses its nose to gather food.

Peter's Spear-Nosed Bat
(Phylloderma stenops)
Mammal (bat family)
Lives: South America
Eats: Insects
Its strange nose squeaks to help it find flying insects.

Camel
(Camelus dromedarius)
Mammal (camel family)
Lives: Africa and Arabia
Eats: Leaves and plants
Can close its nostrils during storms to keep the sand out.

30

Bull
(Bos taurus)
Mammal (cattle/antelope family)
Lives: Worldwide
Eats: Plants
Bulls have rings in their noses
to keep them under control.

Puffin
(Fratercula arctica)
Bird (auk family)
Lives: Atlantic coastal islands
Eats: Fish
It can hold up to 60 small
fish in its colourful beak.

Hippopotamus
(Hippopotamus amphibius)
Mammal (pig/hippopotamus family)
Lives: African swamps and lakes
Eats: Plants
Spends most of its time in
water, submerged up to its nose.

Proboscis Monkey
(Nasalis larvatus)
Mammal (monkey family)
Lives: Borneo jungle
Eats: Mostly plants
Swims well, and is very
noisy.

Features

Index